The more energy, the faster the bits flip. Earth, air,
and water in the end are all made of energy, but the
different forms they take are determined by information. To do anything requires energy. To specify what is
done requires information.

SETH LLOYD, MIT

Programming the Universe (2006)

Given the resources committed to them, the reverence
afforded to those who own them, the adoration of the
"masons" who build them, and the awe for what they house,
datacenters might be called the digital cathedrals of the
twenty-first century. Datacenters do deserve a certain awe.
They constitute a key feature of a system that, as Green-
peace accurately observed, is the "largest thing we [will]
build as a species."

That "thing" is the Cloud, the massive ecosystem of
information-digital hardware. It is society's first new infrastructure in nearly a century.

Civilization is built on foundational infrastructures,
the physical networks that provide society not just with
core services, but the platforms enabling all the other

1

features and services of a modern economy. All infrastructures entail energy and can be thus neatly divided into two general categories: those that consume energy, and those that produce it.

Only three classes of infrastructures produce energy: those responsible for food, for hydrocarbons, and for electricity. The list is similarly short for energy-consuming infrastructures: clean water, transportation, and communications. Notably, 80 percent of our economy is found in the myriad activities associated with the energy-consuming infrastructures. And now, for the first time in a century, we can add a new name to this latter list: the Cloud.

Data has been called the "new oil" and the Internet the "information superhighway." Some analogize the rise of the Internet with the emergence of the electric age. But these analogies don't properly capture what is now underway with the Cloud and especially its most prominent (and ineptly named) feature, artificial intelligence.

The emerging Cloud is as different from the communications infrastructure that preceded it as air travel is different from automobiles. And, using energy as a metric for scale, today's global Cloud already consumes more energy than global aviation.

Stories about digital "disruptions" we've already witnessed only hint at the structural, economic, and social

The world's computer-communications systems now use twice as much electricity as does the country of Japan.

changes yet to come as the Cloud infrastructure expands. Indeed, most of what has happened thus far has been associated with the news, advertising, financial, entertainment, and communications industries – all of those information-centric themselves. But those activities constitute, collectively, less than 20 percent of the GDP. We are still in early days of the "digitalization" of the remaining 80 percent of the economy.

Uber's disintermediation of automobile ownership and taxi use is just one example of the next phase. Everything in the non-information parts of the economy – from construction and agriculture to manufacturing and health-care – is still largely undigitalized by the standards of, say, newspapers, advertising, and entertainment. The Silicon Valley legend Andreessen Horowitz famously said that "software is eating everything." True. But we are only now on the appetizer course.

As we explore in the following pages the new infrastructure through the lens of energy demand, it becomes clear that we live at a time of transformation equivalent to 1919, which was three decades after cars had been invented and only a decade into the era of useful, affordable, personal mobility. The Cloud was "born" only a decade ago, and the first Internet datacenters appeared thirty years ago.

Nonetheless, today's top five Cloud architects (Amazon, Microsoft, Google, Apple, and Facebook; there will be more) are spending over $400 billion annually – a rate rising rapidly – to build out the Cloud infrastructure. And the associated Cloud services in the United States alone (currently the epicenter of construction and investment) already constitute an $80 billion annual business, exceeding the annual revenues for all U.S. freight railroad services.

On the horizon, one should expect an array of new services that are no more imaginable today than Twitter, Uber, or Airbnb were in 1990. In due course, the Cloud, like all infrastructures before it, will evolve into a "critical infrastructure." Policymakers and regulators will be increasingly tempted – or enjoined – to engage issues of competition, fairness, and even social disruptions, along with the challenges of abuse of market power, both valid and trumped up.

We already see governments wrestling with the disruptions to news distribution and personal privacy. One can look to history for guidance on the nature, if not the specifics, of what to expect from policymakers and regulators as new technologies continue to plow through society. The invention of radio created an entirely novel means for promulgating news, changing velocity and reach as well as profit models. Policymakers reacted by creating an entirely new regulatory regime, starting with the 1927 Federal Radio Commission that President Roosevelt expanded into the Federal Communications Commission (FCC) in 1934. Similarly, safety concerns following the invention of air travel brought us the National Transportation Safety Board, an entirely new infrastructure (epitomized by the airport), and a new metric for personal travel, air-miles.

The metric used to gauge the hyperbolic growth of our digital age? Bits and bytes of data. Every 30 seconds the global Internet transports and processes a greater quantity of data than found in the Library of Congress. And both data generation and the software tools to refine that raw material are still accelerating. But analogies to libraries' worth of data – or words like petabytes and zettabytes of traffic, or impressive trillion-dollar stock market valuations – fail to properly illuminate the sheer scale of the underlying hardware.

At the beating heart of the World Wide Web's virtuality we find something more familiar: huge buildings called datacenters where data is stored, processed, and massaged. For real estate firms that track and monetize such buildings, they're just warehouses filled with logic

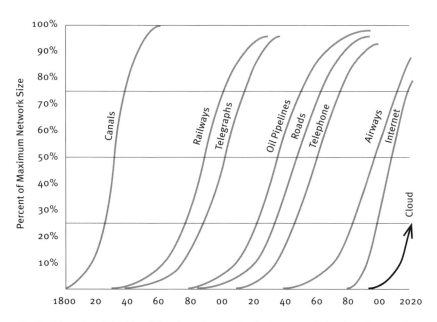

Derived from Arnulf Grübler, "Time for a Change: On the Patterns of Diffusion of Innovation," *Daedalus*, Vol. 125, No. 3, "The Liberation of the Environment" (Summer, 1996).

engines and digital hardware instead of, say, skyscrapers filled with people and furniture. Both add efficiency to commerce and propel prosperity, and both epitomize the dawn of their respective eras. Skyscrapers emerged at the turn of twentieth century, datacenters at the turn of the twenty-first.

But datacenters utterly eclipse skyscrapers in every other measure. The power of the companies that own and operate them has already – even in these early days of the Cloud's ascendancy – ignited both awe and opprobrium. And the quantity of capital and energy that datacenters consume is unprecedented. The world's computer-communications systems now use twice as much electricity as does the country of Japan.

Yet, as far-reaching as the Cloud has already become, we are at the end of the beginning – *not the beginning of the end* – of what the digital masons are building.

Digital-infrastructure masons caught between profit seeking and virtue shaming

Six years ago Google held a conference at its headquarters' campus entitled "How Green Is The Internet?" Other tech companies and researchers have explored this same question. It is of course a question directly derivative from the fact of the scale of the Cloud and its remarkable energy appetite. Google now reports that, since that conference, its direct use of electricity has at least tripled – a torrid growth rate typical of Cloud companies – but *not* typical in the rest of the economy.

Now the issue is more than just how much power datacenters themselves consume. Many Cloud companies are engaged in the debate over how society itself is fueled, and over the future of the grids that all businesses and consumers share.

7

Early in 2019, Google touted that for the previous two years the company had achieved "100 percent renewable energy." This is not to single out Google; many other tech firms make similar claims, not least Apple and Facebook. The problem with such a public claim is simple reality: datacenters and the Cloud can no more run on wind and solar than an aircraft can fly by burning wood. While wind and solar energy can produce the electricity that silicon engines need, just as wood produces heat that is the essence of jet propulsion, neither can produce energy in the form that the systems actually require. An aircraft requires a high-density fuel. A datacenter requires always-on power.

Today, wind and solar together supply about 9 percent of all electricity while two-thirds comes from natural gas and coal. The latter two enable an always-on grid. Only by regulatory legerdemain or rhetorical obfuscation could one claim that any part of the Cloud is 100 percent powered by wind and solar.

How, then, do they? The regulatory "fix" is hidden in plain sight. Companies are permitted to purchase Renewable Energy Credits (not the kilowatt-hours themselves) from a wind or solar farm and then "attach" those credits to a facility somewhere else that consumes grid power which is available 24/7 – not just when it's windy or sunny. Similarly, any company can engage in a Power Purchase Agreement (PPA) to fund the construction of wind/solar farms to supply electricity to the grid, and then take credit for that green output as a kind of "offset" to the power actually consumed. (To be fair, Google does state – below the headline, literally – that its 100 percent renewable claim is based on such "offsets" and not in fact on what actually energizes its facilities.)

The "availability" of a power source is not a semantic nicety. It is a specific and critical technical feature. Any company could, whether operating a datacenter or daycare center, opt to disconnect from the grid and build an independent stand-alone green power system. The impediment is cost: building such a system to supply 24/7 power would cost nearly 400 percent more than grid power.

Exploring the claim that the overall energy economy will, or even can, undergo a near-term migration to become 100 percent wind/solar-powered is beyond this book's scope. But note that Google's own engineers published an analysis of renewable energy at scale which

A single smartphone's annual pro rata energy use—in the network, not in your hand—amounts to as much electricity as a modern household refrigerator.

concluded that the technologies to make it competitive with conventional energy in terms of cost and availability "haven't been invented yet."

As to whether our society's grids should be radically restructured, Google asserts: "To bridge the gap between intermittent renewable resources and the constant demands of the digital economy, we'll have to test new business models, deploy new technologies, and advocate for new policies." Any Cloud company is welcome to try any business model, and all would be welcome to join in funding basic R&D to find new energy technologies. But advocacy for "new policies" properly falls in the public domain and intersects with countless other businesses and citizens with needs and rights pertaining to grid cost and reliability.

Regardless of how electricity is produced, however, the far more interesting story is in how the Cloud has emerged as a major and fast-growing energy-consuming infrastructure. The entire ecosystem associated with the Cloud likely already consumes about 10 percent of global electricity. And many forecasts – not just this one – see that share rising, perhaps by as much as twofold over the coming two decades.

National debates of this kind emerge only episodically, at times when deep structural changes are underway in the economy. The age of railroads yielded consequences analogous to our time. Railroads did more than revolutionize travel and commerce while triggering the first great rise in global energy consumption; they determined where telegraph lines and oil pipelines were routed, and where and how towns and businesses were built.

The velocity and nature of railroads even spawned modern time zones and the popularity of personal watches. Rail's reach and radical cost reductions transformed agriculture and demographics, permanently moving westward the epicenter of the nation's "breadbasket." Rail changed the nature of commerce itself, inspiring Richard Sears, in 1893, to create a retail giant that would last more than a century. Rail brought manifold economic and social benefits to the public, as well as outsized wealth for its architects.

Because of all that power and wealth, the railroads also generated social and political debate, riots, and massive media preoccupation with the so-called "robber barons," an invective coined by a journalist at the time. Apropos the current debate over market and monopoly power, the most important single consequence from the rise of the rail age was that Congress, reacting to the combination of perceived and real abuses in 1887, created the first modern regulatory agency (and progenitor of all subsequent ones): the Interstate Commerce Commission (ICC).

The excesses of the barons of that era, both real and imagined, were followed by excessive regulatory intrusions. By World War I, regulators had so damaged the economic and structural viability of the rail industry that, in 1917, President Woodrow Wilson nationalized it. Railroads returned, badly damaged, to private hands three years later with a phalanx of new regulations.

Analogies are never perfect, but they're instructive. And in every era the lessons from history always seem "old fashioned" and "out of date" compared to the magic of technology of that day. We are again at a magic moment in history.

Defining structures of epochs: cathedrals, skyscrapers, and datacenters

The Middle Ages marked civilization's first epoch of industrialization. The gear, pulley, water wheel, and windmill – and, late in that age, the clock – all propelled an unprecedented rate of economic progress and human wellbeing. This wealth and technological prowess enabled the construction of the great cathedrals – the tallest buildings that humanity had ever built to occupy. The cathedrals' architects and masons were revered. Six centuries would pass before humanity saw a building exceed the 524-foot tower of England's Lincoln Cathedral, completed in 1311.

The skyscraper was the icon of the next industrial revolution. In the early 1900s, enabled by the technologies of steel, steam, and electricity, builders were finally able to exceed the height of the great cathedrals. In 1913, *The New York Times* called Manhattan's new skyscraper, the 792-foot Woolworth Building, then the world's tallest building, a "cathedral of commerce." Skyscrapers amplified the economic power of urban cores. But because each was a vertical city in its own right, they also entailed the prodigious consumption of materials and energy.

Today it's the datacenter that is the icon of the next revolution, enabled by the age of silicon, software, and glass fiber. The insufficiently evocative term "datacenter" emerged in the 1970s to describe proliferating rooms full of computers. That's equivalent to calling a skyscraper an "office center." Modern datacenters bear as much resemblance to '70s computer rooms as the three-thousand-foot Burj Khalifa in Dubai, the world's tallest skyscraper, does to a dry goods store in Tombstone, Arizona.

The world's biggest datacenter (so far) is located near Reno, Nevada, and has under its roof twice the square footage as does the Burj Khalifa. The latter is configured to house about 100,000 bio-processors (a.k.a. humans), each of which, not incidentally, generates about 100 watts of heat. Meanwhile, the datacenter houses some 200,000 silicon processers, each of which is also roughly 100 watts.

While both classes of building cost roughly the same per square foot to build, far more datacenters are under construction. But a square foot of a datacenter rents for five time as much as a skyscraper. This explains why datacenters attract real estate investors. And in resource terms, a square foot of datacenter inhales 100 times as much electricity as does a square foot of skyscraper. Consequently, datacenter firms often talk about their buildings in terms of megawatts.

But counting square feet remains a visually convenient way to compare the scales of these two epoch-defining icons at the beginning of our epoch. The ten biggest datacenters in the world contain more square footage collectively than do the top ten skyscrapers. And there are more than five thousand enterprise-class datacenters in the world, compared to about 1,500 enterprise-class "office centers," i.e., skyscrapers taller than forty stories. Meanwhile, there are another eight million small datacenters in the world.

And this is just the beginning. While there are only a handful of skyscrapers at the scale of the Burj Khalifa in existence and planned, there are already about four hundred hyperscale datacenters globally (each with more than a million square feet under roof) with another one hundred more expected in just a couple of years.

Already, datacenters alone are estimated collectively to consume 2 percent of the world's electricity. This means datacenters use about 30-fold more kilowatt-hours than

Economists and pundits generally underestimate infrastructure-anchored transformations.

the world's four million electric cars consume today. In the future, when there are 30 times more electric vehicles (EVs), they'll use as much electricity as *today's* datacenters – but by then, global demand for still more datacenters will have blown well past demand for EVs.

A full decade ago, Google's engineers anticipated this hyperscale trend in a prescient research document, *The Datacenter as a Computer: An Introduction to the Design of Warehouse-Scale Machines*, which classified a one-million-square-foot datacenter not as a building full of computers but as a single monstrous multi-megawatt-class (warehouse-scale) computer (WSC). As those Google engineers observed a decade ago: "Energy efficiency is a key cost driver for WSCs and we expect energy usage to become an increasingly important factor of WSC design."

In 2008, a Department of Energy (DOE) report on datacenter energy use in America showed that those buildings used a quantity of electricity that already rivaled that used by the entire U.S. chemical industry. The DOE published an update in 2016 concluding that total U.S. datacenter energy demand had remained essentially unchanged between 2010 and 2014, having grown 24 percent from 2005 to 2010, and 90 percent from 2000 to 2005. That report reached the conclusion that datacenter energy use had thus entered a kind of new normal where data use proliferates but datacenter energy use stays essentially flat or might even decline.

The DOE conclusion, however, failed on two counts. It failed to anticipate the emergence of Cloud computing and hyperscale, as well as the digital market forces driving them. And it suffered from the common error of basing forecasts on trends seen during a recession. From 2008 until 2014, capital investments in hardware of all kind slowed, including spending on both datacenters and digitalization. In 2017, however, shortly after the 2016 DOE update was issued, datacenter capital spending rose at double the 2016 rate, and eclipsed the prior three years of spending combined. Over the five years following 2014, the total square footage of datacenters announced for construction tripled the annual rate of the previous decade.

In addition, during the recession-constrained period of modest expansion, datacenter operators focused on energy efficiency. But that produced mostly one-time gains, equivalent to, say, replacing a traditional light bulb with an LED. Most of the "low hanging fruit" in energy efficiency has been harvested.

This is the central question: will future demand for Cloud services grow faster than gains in energy efficiency? If so, then overall Cloud energy demand will rise.

The answer, at a high-level of abstraction, is found in Roger Fouquet's seminal book *Heat, Power and Light: Revolutions in Energy Services*. Fouquet mapped five centuries of trends between 1500 and 2000 for the four core energy-consuming services that improved human well-being: transport, power, heat (for buildings and manufacturing), and light. Fouquet's central conclusion:

> *A key idea in the book is the tendency for markets to find ways of consuming energy more efficiently, producing ever-cheaper energy services and, in the long run, consuming greater amounts of energy.*

Fouquet showed how efficiencies improved continuously – and even radically – in each energy-service domain. He also showed that by 1850 society used as much energy for transportation as was used for heat a century earlier. Similarly, by 1950 illumination used as much energy as transportation had in 1850. If the pattern continues, by 2050 society will use more energy for data than was used for illumination in 1950.

Fouquet could have included information services, mapping energy costs associated with building libraries and making paper, and later with the telegraph and telephone. But these earlier information systems accounted for miniscule energy use. The ignition point, when the energy cost of information began to rise, occurred roughly when Fouquet's history ends.

A single smartphone's annual pro rata energy use – in the network, not in your hand – amounts to as much electricity as a modern household *refrigerator*. That reality is easy to derive from the fact that today's 3.5 billion smartphones are responsible for about 60 percent of all Internet traffic, and thus about that share of energy used by all global digital systems.

Just as a refrigerator's locus of energy is at remote power plants, so is a smartphone's and that of other IT tools, from autonomous cars to artificial intelligence. Similarly, just as power systems require transmission lines and cars require highways, the Cloud requires its own "highway." The "information superhighway" is unique, however, and as different from telephones as paved roads are different from canals.

The invisible and voracious "information superhighway"

In a 1974 essay, the Korean-American artist Nam June Paik popularized the term "information superhighway," which Al Gore would later borrow in a 1978 congressional speech. America had just experienced two decades of prosperity as the interstate superhighways became, in Paik's words, "the backbone for ... economic growth."

But Paik's insights went beyond nomenclature. Consider his predictions, bearing in mind they predated the Internet by over a decade:

> The mass entertainment TV as we see it now will be divided into, or rather gain many branches and tails of, differentiated video cultures. Picture phone, tele-facsimile, two-way inter-active TV for shopping, libraryresearch, opinionpolling, healthconsultation, bio-communication, inter-office data transmission and many other variants will turn the TV set into the expanded mixed media telephone system for

thousands and one new applications, not only for daily convenience but also for the enrichment of life itself.

Paik got a lot right. What he got wrong were the energy implications.

He believed that the information superhighway would "drastically reduce air travel, and ... the chaotic shuttling of airport buses through city streets – forever!" In fact, air traffic has risen nearly 1,000 percent since his forecast, and road traffic has ballooned – including, in no small irony, freight traffic because of two-day delivery services. The Internet turned out to be an economic accelerant for global commerce, increasing rather than decreasing travel.

Then there are the collateral, or induced, energy features of new Cloud-enabled services. The popularity of Paik's predicted "inter-active TV for shopping" and rapid two-day (and now same-day) delivery with e-commerce has spawned an enormous increase in warehouse construction and on-road truck miles. Delivering goods individually to consumers' homes instead of in bulk on pallets to central locations (shopping malls) is more convenient. It's also more energy-intensive.

Paik also offered an energy trope that is still common; i.e., that video teleconferences somehow consume little

The pursuit of machines to save labor and to create new services and comforts is as old as civilization.

energy, or as Paik thought, "no energy." It's true that beaming a video signal on a radio wave uses less energy than propelling an automobile or aircraft. But *all* things, including transporting information, use energy.

Total energy use on any highway, paved or photonic, comes from the combination of distance and frequency of travel. From the telegraph to the telephone and wireless radio and TV, engineers have continuously found ways to move more information with greater efficiency and speed, over far greater distances. While all the world's physical highways collectively span some 20 million miles – if stretched out they'd reach one-fourth the way to our sun – the information superhighway is astronomically bigger. The world's 4 million cell towers connect billions of people on an invisible network that is effectively 100 *billion* miles long. That'd take you to the sun and back 500 times.

The wireless highways are to wired networks what trucks are to railroads: synergistic. Fixed networks (rail, fiber) can carry enormous volumes with great efficiency. But it's the flexibility of local distribution via wireless for data, and trucks for freight, that catalyzes profoundly greater utility and economic leverage. In both cases, flexibility entails a higher energy cost per unit of goods transported.

For trucks that's obvious. To understand why it's so with a radio, imagine trying to fill a bucket with a sprinkler instead of a hose. Wireless instead of wired networks entail an almost 10-fold increase in energy consumed per unit of data transported. There is a similar, though slightly lower, energy penalty per pound-mile for trucks versus rail. The pattern: greater energy use is a measure and a consequence of superior utility and economic value.

The world's cellular networks collectively use over $20 billion of electricity each year, or between 200 and 300 billion kilowatt-hours. That's also roughly the same quantity of electricity that the world's datacenters used a few years ago, or as much electricity as the country of Italy uses for all purposes. It's the quantity of energy consumed by all of California's automobiles each year.

Radios have always been power hungry. In 1902, when Guglielmo Marconi built the first radio station to broadcast a commercial wireless signal, it was energized by a several-hundred-kilowatt coal-fired power plant. Engineers knew from day one that shrinking physical and energy footprints was key to creating radio networks. By World War I, portable radios weighed a mere ton and could be drawn on a horse-cart. By World War II, Motorola delivered the iconic thirty-five-pound back-pack radio for GIs. By 1984, the year Apple announced its Macintosh, Motorola released the world's first cell phone. At $9,000 (today's dollars), that two-pound "brick" with a thirty-minute talk time was a portent of what would follow.

By the 1980s, engineers had collapsed the energy appetite and size of radios down to finger-nail-sized chips that, combined with a grid of radio "cells" – a 1947 idea conceived at Bell Labs – ignited the cell *phone* revolution. But it took nearly two more decades for Apple's iPhone to trigger the wireless mobile revolution. Within a half-dozen years of the iPhone's 2007 release, the world had more smartphones than smart desktops. And voice doesn't account for even 1 percent of today's smartphone traffic. Today's wireless traffic is greater than the entire wired Internet in 2013, when the age of Cloud infrastructure really began.

Even as abstemiously efficient as are the radio chipsets in a smartphone, they use about 40 percent of the onboard battery's power. (The screen and logic circuits use the rest in roughly equal proportions.) And because the radios in smartphones are low-power (to increase operating time), they have limited range. The utility of smartphones is made possible by placing millions of far more powerful radios – cellular "base stations" – close enough to every possible mobile location to ensure a seamless network. Unlike other infrastructures, the Cloud's network is a major energy user itself. The energy impact of going from voice landlines to mobile Cloud services is equivalent to switching from bicycles to SUVs.

The Cloud itself accelerates the demand for data precisely because of the "magic" of services like Uber, virtual assistants, real-time language translation, or increasingly real-time anything. The average smartphone user voluntarily pays $1,000 annually in toll charges to use the "information superhighway." Part of those tolls includes a fuel charge.

Hans Thirring may have been the first person to think about the aggregate energy used by radios. In his seminal 1958 book, *Energy for Man*, Thirring estimated that the tens of thousands of broadcast towers of that day used about 0.1 percent of America's electricity. But neither Thirring, nor Marconi earlier, imagined the network we have today.

So what comes next? The future of the Cloud – and its energy appetite – depends on how much digital magic yet emerges. Economists and pundits generally underestimate infrastructure-anchored transformations.

We can glimpse the shape of the future by looking at what innovators have recently invented but has yet to be fully commercialized. The two new core tech trends are the same as those that brought us to where we are now: more efficient radios, and greater traffic capacity and speed on the networks.

Expanding and accelerating the "information superhighway" with 5G

Engineers have continued to shrink the size and energy appetite of radios, even down to dust-mote size, enabling entirely new kinds of connections in nearly any product, machine, or thing, including our bodies. Some classes of embedded radios can even power themselves without wires or batteries by harvesting infinitesimal amounts of energy available in the ambient environment. The key effect of all this is to radically extend the reach and scale of the invisible superhighway. It's on track to expand again by as much as it did when we went from landlines to wireless.

Speed, or more properly, bandwidth, is the second feature that matters to all highways and networks. Just as fiber optics vaulted speed/bandwidth far past what traditional copper cable could handle, we now have the emergence of semiconductor radio chipsets with millimeter-wave 5G capabilities. 5G creates a step-change as significant as the shift two decades ago from slow analog to high-speed digital radio networks.

In the ineffable physics of electromagnetic waves,

speed and bandwidth come with using shorter wavelengths. (wavelength is inversely proportional to frequency.) The 5G millimeter waves are, tautologically, far shorter than the nearly meter-long waves used by the first cellular radios, and nearly a millionfold shorter than the several-hundred-meter-long radio waves Marconi first launched. Millimeter wavelengths (i.e., thousands of MHz,

Once there's a general-purpose supercomputer, we'll see far more of them than cruise ships.

or GHz) can handle traffic at the speed of first-generation fiber optics, effectively unlocking fiber-speed over the air.

What follows from all this? Count on a massive proliferation of hardware to build more superhighways. Best estimates see the 5G rollout requiring over seventy million small-cell base stations installed in urban and industrial environments within a half-dozen years: a more than 10-fold increase over today's total base station count. A century ago each household had one radio; we'll soon have hundreds and even thousands of radios *per person*, thus weaving a network of unprecedented proportions. The term "information highway" loses salience. The near future is one of ambient high-speed connectivity as accessible as the air we breathe.

The combination of ubiquity with speed and bandwidth unlocks not only high-resolution streaming video – for better or worse, high-definition TV on-demand, anywhere, anytime – but also the kind of performance necessary for augmented and virtual reality, as well as for a new range of autonomous devices, from drones and self-driving cars to collaborative robots and artificial intelligence. All require near-instantaneous access to the Cloud's supercomputing capacity.

And what exactly will people do with such capabilities? By now, we should have at least some glimmer of what's coming – having so recently experienced the transition from the tethered desktop Internet to today's mobile network.

For starters, there will be a lot more video entertainment. Netflix, Disney, Google (YouTube), Microsoft, Facebook, and all the related video purveyors certainly think so. Entertainment is one of humanity's oldest industries, one that invariably expands with wealth and leisure. (Over two-thirds of all airline passengers travel for leisure and entertainment, not business.) 5G enables vital applications too, especially augmented and virtual reality tools which will transform much more than retail and entertainment, but also manufacturing, construction, mining, energy production, agriculture, and – likely, ultimately the biggest market – healthcare and medicine.

The net effect of all the new services and products will be, as has always been the case for every infrastructure in its early days, a rapid and even faster-than-forecast rise in traffic. Consider that in 2010, one industry consortium forecast that mobile traffic would increase 89-fold by 2020. Instead, Cisco now expects traffic will have risen by at least 160-fold by 2021 compared to 2010. Traffic consumes fuel.

This intersection of digital mobility and the Cloud creates the defining infrastructure of our time, as automotive mobility and highways were in the last century. Gasoline consumption by cars rose some 700 percent over the decades of the automotive infrastructure's expansion, only recently leveling off. Fuel use on the information superhighway has just begun.

Experts in the community of digital masons know that network power is "one of the most important, yet underappreciated aspects of the next generation cellular network." Technical plans already exist to reduce by 98 percent the energy needed to transport a byte. That sounds like a big improvement, and it would be if we were talking about automobiles and airplanes. But in the world of bytes, such gains are business-as-usual and swamped by the far greater rise in traffic.

Even assuming rapid adoption of optimal efficiencies,

global wireless networks are forecast to spend over $90 billion a year on electricity by 2025, a more than fourfold increase from where we are now. The actual number may turn out to be far larger. A data tsunami is coming. And not counted in today's traffic forecasts are the impacts from artificial intelligence (AI) and robots.

Are CAFÉ-like fuel efficiency standards on the horizon for AI and robots?

Now that the age of artificial intelligence is finally in sight after decades of research, it remains widely misunderstood and, inevitably, overhyped. Polls reveal many Americans seem to fear "the machine." For that we can blame Hollywood mythology and the coterie of pundits claiming AI means the end of work.

Of course computers outperform people in many tasks. Cars also outperform humans and horses. The pursuit of machines to save labor and to create new services and comforts is as old as civilization. But cars are not artificial horses any more than jets are artificial birds – or AI is "artificial intelligence." In the Venn diagrams of real-world functionalities, these all overlap but are profoundly different. As have all machines over history, AI will change the nature of work. But overall employment and the economy will grow. (For a longer rebuttal of dystopian claims, see my 2018 book, *Work in the Age of Robots*.)

AI is now emerging from the maturation of three symbiotic silicon domains: ubiquitous sensors generating massive data (the raw material), a new class of logic chips that doesn't calculate but estimates, and of course the high-performance communication networks carrying raw data one way and delivering "refinements" the other. It's no coincidence that this architecture emulates humans: a distributed sensory apparatus, a brain, and a labyrinthine nervous system.

As with human intelligence, energy use by AI is a feature, not a bug. In fact, AI comprises the most data-intensive – and thus energy-intensive – use of computers in history. With AI, one can ask interesting questions: how much energy will it take for a computer to *navigate* a vehicle driving someone to work, or to compose a symphony, or to discover a new drug? We're not talking about the energy used to propel a car, or light a concert hall or laboratory. Instead the question is about the energy needed by the artificial brains themselves.

When an all-robocar future does arrive, the energy used just by all the automotive AI "brains" under car hoods will alone burn more fuel than all the cars on

California roads today. Put differently, the energy needed for silicon navigation logic and sensing will degrade a vehicle's propulsion fuel mileage by as much as 10 percent, possibly more.

Measured in Detroit rather than Silicon Valley terms, a robocar's brain operates at about 150 mpg. That may sound impressive but it's at least 1,000 times less efficient than the average *natural*, if addled, brain. When it comes to employing human intelligence we usually count dollars, but we do know the energy cost of neurons. The astoundingly efficient "wetware" cossetted within the human cranium runs on just 12 watts.

Your brain doesn't consume a hundredth of a kilowatt-hour (kWh) while you drive to work; in car terms, the brain gets at least 150,000 mpg. That assumes fully half of your brain is devoted to navigation (doubtless an overestimate) while the other half multi-tasks listening to podcasts or chatting, or daydreaming. A composer's brain engaged during the days it takes to write a movie score burns about 10 kWh. And we can impute some 1,000 kWh burned collectively by the brains of a dozen researchers working, say, for five years to discover a new drug. These are all trivial quantities of energy. But we humans are eager to amplify such tasks, and many more, with silicon.

The voracious appetite of "cognitive" software is not news to AI engineers. FedEx's development of autonomous wheeled robots for local deliveries is based on Dean Kamen's human-guided iBot, a sophisticated self-propelled stair-climbing wheelchair. But as Kamen recently observed, the energy appetite of silicon navigation will "reduce the range substantially." Such fuel-burning local delivery robots deployed on sidewalks – already common in warehouses – will be deployed long before autonomous cars dominate highways. For on-road robocars, there remains much to be conquered in safety, reliability, integration, and liability areas.

Before delving into AI's future, consider the claims that robocars will lead to overall energy savings because, in effect, autonomous vehicles will drive more efficiently. But citizens will one day embrace robocars not for efficiency but for convenience, comfort, and safety. Such attributes increase energy use: e.g., more frequent and faster trips in vehicles that are bigger (for sleeping?) and heavier. Models that "prove" energy savings all assume inverse behaviors: slower driving and shared rides in smaller vehicles.

In addition, not only will robocars increase energy use by chauffeuring millions who can't drive (young, old, infirm, etc.), analyses of behavior and convenience suggest that robocars will also "induce" new energy-using behaviors. The net effect will increase total U.S. vehicle-miles by an amount equal to twice those driven by all Californians today.

So far, AI's energy implications remain largely a practical concern for engineers, the infrastructure masons of the twenty-first century. That's not surprising. No attention was afforded the energy cost of the Internet circa 1979. Similarly, in 1958 when Pan Am began passenger jet service, or in 1908 when Ford introduced the Model T, no one discussed future fuel use from flying and driving. And as energy use rose, the pursuit of efficiency inevitably followed, because that's the key to unlocking the commercial viability and social value of new infrastructures. But the net effect has always been more overall energy use.

The architecture and appetite of artificial intelligence

The practical and energy implications of AI are revealed in its essential difference from conventional computing. That difference was best captured nearly sixty years ago by the MIT computer scientist J. C. Licklider, who wrote: "Present-day computers are designed primarily to solve pre-formulated problems." The future, he forecast, would "bring the computing machine effectively into the formulative parts of technical problems" and the "processes of thinking that must go on in 'real time,' time that moves too fast to permit using computers in conventional ways."

Licklider was summarizing the profound difference between a computer program that *calculates* and software that *estimates* an outcome based on continuous awareness of and response to information about physical events in the real world, in real time. That difference manifests itself in the nature of the underlying silicon logic that can perform "machine learning" rather than "information processing."

Rather than a central processing unit (CPU) measured by the speed of linearly executed logic operations, AI is anchored in graphic processing units (GPUs, and similarly named alternatives) where speed is measured in terms of running massively parallel comparisons of, say, graphic images. AI-class chips account for 80 percent of all growth forecast for semiconductor logic sales over the coming half-dozen years, becoming a $70 billion annual market.

Given that humans are so visually oriented, and so much of reality is represented visually, consider that while a 100 watt CPU may look at as many as 1,000 images per

Untethered robots, whether winged, wheeled, or walking, are bound by the same energy architecture as humans.

second, a 500 watt GPU can blow through 25,000 images per second. GPUs are thus far more energy efficient per image processed. But because the real world is a prolific image generator, the GPU doesn't end up saving energy, but instead enables new applications and thus more energy consumption.

Thus a car's trunk full of GPUs and CPUs (the latter still needed for non-image logic and control functions) can easily create at least a 2,000 W load that must run constantly, not least because, self-evidently, a "sleep" mode is not desirable with a navigation computer. A 2 kW load constitutes about 10 to 20 percent of the power an engine needs to keep a car rolling at cruise.

Meanwhile, a building full of 17,000 GPUs interconnected with 8,000 CPUs, known as a supercomputer, consumes 12 megawatts (MW). That's enough power to drive a cruise ship. Last year, the 12 MW Summit, currently the world's most powerful supercomputer, came on-line at a 200 petaflop speed, enabling America to recapture from China the performance record for such machines. Once there's a general-purpose supercomputer, we'll see far more of them than cruise ships.

But the world still awaits the next leap in AI compute capability. When it comes to running a physics-based model of even the simplest molecular behaviors, today's supercomputers churn for hours, even days, to simulate mere seconds of reality. In order to simulate "virtual" human organs to test drugs "*in silico*" (an actual term) we need machines a thousandfold more powerful. And such beasts are on the near-term horizon.

The Department of Energy has issued contracts to three teams to each build an "exascale" supercomputer, a thousandfold leap over petaflop machines. Only six years ago, engineers worried that this next leap in super-computing would lead to a single machine demanding 500 MW. But efficiency gains will allow a more-than-tenfold jump in compute horsepower over today's #1 machine with a "mere" threefold to fourfold rise in power demand. Frontier, the first exascale machine expected to be online in two years, will clock in at "only" 40 MW. Then the next plateau is a zetascale machine, another thousandfold jump which perhaps will "only" need 100 MW.

Meanwhile, in the here and now, everyday businesses don't have to wait to queue up for supercomputing processor time; Google has announced it will rent out time on its 100-petaflop capability in the Cloud, homegrown with custom GPUs. Until just over a year ago, getting access to 100 petaflops was only feasible by waiting for time on a handful of special-purpose government-owned machines. The

democratization of true general-purpose AI has begun.
Scaling and lower costs will result from Cloud providers
offering AI as a service.

Supercomputers and AI supercharge the Cloud

It's as hard to imagine all the uses for petascale AI as it
was in 1987 to image all the uses for the PC, and similarly
in 2007 with the smartphone. Both would change the
landscape. AI can do much more than speech and facial
recognition, both considered "low precision" tasks requiring relatively little compute horsepower. (Single AI
chipsets can already perform such tasks in handhelds.)
But simulating driving and flying conditions, whether to
train or navigate autonomous vehicles, or reading x-rays or
simulating drug interactions in human cells, are high precision tasks. Those tasks call for petaflop and exaflop
machines.

Investors are already eagerly pursuing AI for what it
might offer in their Sisyphean hope to beat the "invisible
hand" of the stock market. But for most citizens, AI's benefits will mean such things as better forecasts of natural
events like weather and earthquakes, and far better medical diagnostics. And exascale in particular will enable

researchers to plumb the depths of nature and simulate molecular behavior *in silico* in pursuit of novel materials, medicines, or discoveries in basic sciences yet unanticipated.

On the industrial front, AI startups are promising radical gains in production and operational efficiency in every sector, even in fundamental domains such as the design of entirely new kinds of metal alloys optimized for specific purposes, or for next-generation 3D metal printers. Gartner forecasts that the overall global value of AI-derived business activities – Amazon and Google are, so far, essentially CPU-derived – will reach over $4 trillion a year in just a few years.

One *could* measure AI-driven discovery and economic growth in kilowatt-hours per dollar. The learning phase of developing a single AI software application can consume more energy than do fifty cars a year. Or, for example, if in order to accelerate drug discovery just one research team runs only a dozen petascale simulations: that would use the energy equivalent of flying a jumbo jet to Asia. In a future with tens of thousands of AI supercomputers continually simulating and emulating nearly everything, the collective fuel use would easily exceed all global aviation.

Shock and awe as déjà vu all over again

Facebook has already flagged AI as a "major culprit" in the annual doubling of its overall datacenter power use. And that's just to deploy today's nascent AI to perform economically useful but (truth be told) relatively trivial social media and advertising missions. It is of course inherently difficult at this stage to make precise forecasts for the GPU-driven AI revolution. But one can predict the shape and direction of change based on lessons from analogous trajectories driven by the "engines" of previous revolutions: the CPU and even the vacuum tube.

The vacuum tube, invented by John Fleming in 1904, drove the first electronic age. As it happens, vacuum tubes improved at a rate nearly identical to the so-called Moore's Law scaling for CPUs. Ever-more power-dense vacuum tubes (i.e., fundamentally more efficient) yielded a proliferation of devices like radios, stereos, and TVs, as well as massive centralized facilities such as broadcast stations and radars. Vacuum tubes gave us the first electronic

Humanity now fabricates 1,000 times more transistors annually than the entire world grows grains of wheat and rice combined.

computers too – the 1945 ENIAC's room full of 17,000 vacuum tubes gobbled 170 kW.

By 1927, radio sets consumed one third of all household spending on furniture. (That ratio, not coincidentally, is roughly the same as today's share of household spending on the wireless Web). As for velocity, radio's trajectory was every bit as fast as we've seen for smartphones: the number of homes with radios jumped 10-fold from 1921 to 1927, and then 10-fold again before World War II, when nearly every home had a radio. Radio broadcast stations, the functional equal of today's datacenters, proliferated by the thousands.

Vacuum tube technology also propelled wealth and worries in those days. RCA was the most heavily traded stock on the NYSE and rose over ten thousand percent in the half-dozen years leading up to the 1929 market crash. Newspaper advertising and money rushed into radio. Politicians embraced it. In 1929, Franklin Roosevelt, then the Governor of New York, instituted a weekly "fireside chat" broadcast in order to talk directly to the people, bypassing pesky reporters. People gushed about how, with radio, "isolation had been broken, knowledge and leisure were being flattened," redolent of headlines today about how, for example, "Facebook Has Flattened Human Communication."

And the government, eager to control the new monopolists of radio waves, created in 1926 the Federal Radio Commission (later to become the FCC). Hyperbole and anxiety over tech-driven media disruption were common then as now – from the pernicious impact of intrusive radio broadcasts on social norms to the easy propagation of fake news. In one of history's most amusing examples of the latter, a 1938 radio show by the famous broadcaster Orson Welles, reading from H. G. Wells's *The War of the Worlds*, caused literal panic in the streets across America because of the "news" of a Martian invasion. As they say, *plus ça change* . . .

As for what new businesses, services, and disruptions the more recent invention of the CPU unleashed, that is now well-plowed territory and the source of many modern anxieties. But at the dawn of the CPU age, circa 1970, did anyone see the shape of the future? Perhaps the science fiction writer Arthur C. Clarke, who imagined that over two billion people would one day each own a handheld device with the compute power of 10,000 mainframes.

You can watch a 1974 interview with Clarke, only three years after Intel's IPO, held in a noisy computer room (a.k.a. datacenter). Clarke predicted the collapse in size and the consequent ubiquity of the computing we see today. If Clarke were alive today, what might he predict AI will yet unleash?

Robocars are coming, but robots eat too

It's easy to forecast smarter, bigger datacenters. That's already happening and will be accelerated by AI pods located in both datacenters and on the "edges" of the network, likely at cell towers. And predicting robocars doesn't take much imagination either. Transitioning to them isn't nearly as revolutionary as going from newspapers to radio, or from telephones to smartphones. A robocar is still a car, just with more conveniences and safety, both of which will stimulate more driving.

If Clarke were alive today, it's unlikely he'd be interviewed at Uber or the robocar company, Waymo. Odds are he would suggest Boston Dynamics as a background, with its dog-like robots capable of eerie biomimicry and back-flipping anthropomorphic robots. Or Hanson Robotics, where remarkably human-like and culturally simpatico robots exhibit the capabilities that imagineers and sci-fi writers have envisioned for eons. AI will, finally, unleash the age of general-purpose robots.

Robots will be employed not just in warehouses, but in dangerous labor-centric situations – where there's now a permanent labor shortage. Robots will also be found in agriculture (farmers have long been the first to embrace automation), inspection and security, emergencies, health care (even as companions for the elderly), and, inevitably, for entertainment as well as an array of social and cultural services.

Most robots won't mimic humans and animals (and those that will, will do so for specific, even therapeutic, purposes). The burgeoning field of autonomous machines incudes wheeled and flying drones, and "cobots" on production lines or in operating rooms assisting surgeons. The robot revolution is as inevitable now as was the mobile phone revolution in 2007 and the radio revolution in 1927.

It bears noting at this point that dystopian fears that computers will become smarter than people pre-dates both Hollywood's imagination and even the dawn of modern computing. Ancient Greek myths imagined intelligent automatons. Even in pre-ENIAC days, at the 1939 New York World's Fair, Westinghouse built a stunt robot that walked around with a recorded voice saying: "My brain is bigger than yours." (Westinghouse wanted to show off its automated switchgear used for electric grids.) During World War II, two of the pioneers of modern computing, Claude Shannon and Alan Turing, famously speculated about machine intelligence; hence the "Turing Test."

It is by definition hard to imagine exactly how the era of symbiotic and cognitive computing will unfold, whether with AI infused in the Cloud or in ambulatory digital

Annual global Cloud traffic is today counted at some 40 zettabytes, an impossibly large number to imagine.

assistants. But we can predict with reasonable accuracy that the energy implications will be enormous.

Untethered robots, whether winged, wheeled, or walking, are bound by the same energy architecture as humans. While about 20 percent of a human's on-board fuel system is devoted to the brain, and another 10 to 15 percent to the digestive system in order to convert raw fuel into useful calories, the majority of our fuel budget is consumed by locomotion. Transport uses more energy than cognition. A similar brain-to-transport energy ratio will hold for AI machines.

While Cloud-based AI machines aren't ambulatory, they nonetheless have an energy transport cost associated with acquiring the data that comprises their digital feedstock. Energy is consumed by the networks that connect, collect, and move data from the field. And data traffic is on track to grow at least 100-fold in the coming decade or two.

But it's the ambulatory feature of AI that's new. No one knows how much fuel will be consumed by all the power systems of robots with wheels, wings, and legs that will be used to deliver packages, assist construction workers and nurses, or accompany or comfort an infirm or elderly person. We do know that there's a quiet race underway in materials and mechanical domains to develop break-throughs in propulsion and actuators. But every imaginable artificial system is less efficient than nature's bio-system. A robot moving a pound will use more energy than a human doing it.

From robots and robocars to exascale AI, all this con-stitutes a net new energy demand the world has never seen. One might imagine – Clarke would have – hundreds of mil-lions, perhaps billions, of different classes of AI-enabled automatons. The AI-infused future will add far more energy demand to the world than global aviation – perhaps some-day rivaling all automobiles. And that reality will be a con-sequence of the economic and social value of the services of this new infrastructure.

As next-generation AI finally infuses the 80 percent of the economy largely untouched by automation, the economic benefits will induce activities that are energy-consuming. Wealthier citizens, for example, fly more and buy more vacation homes. There is today of course an industry of analysts who see rising energy use as a prob-lem, not a measure of growth and prosperity.

Those who fear rising energy usage don't (typically) propose stifling the benefits of new energy-consuming services. Instead, the "solution" universally offered is the pursuit – or requirement – of greater efficiency. That "solution" is rhetorically appealing and politically bipartisan. The pursuit of efficiency has been enshrined in myriad existing and proposed laws and regulations. But it won't solve the problem it sets for itself. In fact, on average, efficiency increases energy use.

The relentless pursuit of and confusion over efficiency: Jevons Paradox

The services provided by energy-consuming infrastructures all rely on engines of some kind. Engines convert otherwise useless forms of energy into useful work. And as engineers relentlessly improve efficiencies, markets use those engines more often and in more varied ways. That throughout history this has resulted in *increased* overall energy use is known as the Jevons Paradox.

William Jevons was the British economist who in 1865 codified the so-called "paradox" of efficiency in "The Coal Question," a paper addressing the worry that England could run out of coal and lose the economic benefits of the steam engine. Experts at the time urged more efficient engines to avoid this fate.

Jevons, however, pointed out the fault in this thinking: "It is wholly a confusion of ideas to suppose that the [efficient] use of fuel is equivalent to a diminished consumption ... new modes of [efficiency] will lead to an increase of consumption." Some modern economists call this the "rebound effect," but that term, in effect, gets it backwards. Efficiency is essential for democratizing economically and socially beneficial services – and thus deliberately increasing demand. It's not a "rebound," it's *the* effect.

The purpose of efficiency in the real world, as opposed to the policy world, is to more broadly capture the benefits from an engine. So long as people and businesses want more of those benefits, the declining cost of their use – from efficiency – will increase demand. Any "savings" from less energy per unit of output are more than offset by greater uses for the output.

If steam engines had remained as inefficient as those first invented, they would never have proliferated, nor would there have been the attendant economic growth and rise in coal demand. The same could be said about modern combustion engines. Today's aircraft, for example, are three times more energy-efficient than the first commercial passenger jets. That efficiency didn't "save" fuel compared to early days, but instead propelled a fourfold rise in overall aviation energy use since then.

Only in the policy world do we read government claims that efficiency has "saved" energy by comparing today's energy use with what it would have been absent efficiency improvements. This logic is upside down. Without efficiency gains, the higher costs of the energy-based services would have prevented the rise in energy use.

The microprocessor represents the purest example of this so-called paradox. Over the past sixty years, logic engine energy efficiency has improved over *one billion* fold. No other machine of any kind comes remotely close to matching that.

Consider the implications just from 1980, the Apple II era. A single iPhone operated at 1980 energy-efficiency would require as much power as a Manhattan office building. Similarly, a single data center at 1980 efficiency would require as much power as the entire U.S. grid. In that universe, there wouldn't be any iPhones or datacenters. But *because* of efficiency gains, the world now has billions of smartphones and thousands of skyscraper-class datacenters.

Of course, the Jevons Paradox breaks down in a microeconomic sense. Demand growth for a specific product or service can saturate when limits are hit; e.g., the amount of food a person can eat, or the hours-per-day one individual is willing to drive, or the number of refrigerators or light bulbs per household, etc. In such cases, declining costs have minimal impact on demand. But we're a long way from saturation of anything for over two-thirds of the world.

The ineluctable energy magic of silicon engines

In order to understand why silicon engines have had such astounding energy-efficiency gains compared to combustion engines, and why the Jevons Paradox has a long way to go in digital domains, one has to look to the differences in the nature of the two kinds of engines. One produces information that consumes power, and the other produces power.

Combustion and mechanical engines are designed to effect a physical action. Efficiency is constrained by the immutable laws of thermodynamics, and things like friction, inertia, and gravity. Logic engines, on the other hand, don't produce physical action but are designed to manipulate the *idea* of the numbers zero and one.

And, unlike other engines, logic engines can be accelerated through the clever applications of mathematics, i.e., software. With software one can, for example, employ a trick equivalent to ignoring the white space between useful pixels in a photograph. This is what a compression algorithm does to digitally represent a picture using less data and thus less energy. No such compression option exists in the world of atoms and normal engines.

One consequence of making logic engines both cheaper and more powerful is their soaring production (a variant on the Jevons Paradox). Humanity now fabricates 1,000 times more transistors annually than the entire world grows *grains* of wheat and rice combined.

Or, in economic terms: each year the world's computing manufacturers purchase $300 billion worth of semiconductor engines. That's some 20 to 50 percent more than global spending on the piston engines used to build all the world's wheeled transportation machines. And the former is growing faster than the latter.

The scaling law of transistor-based engines was first codified by the Intel co-founder Gordon Moore in 1965. He wrote that advances in silicon fabrication allowed transistor dimensions to shrink so fast that the number of them per logic engine doubled every two years, and efficiencies followed the same trajectory. While Moore's observation has been enshrined as a "law," it's not a law of nature but a consequence of the nature of logic engines.

Thus, back to Jevons and his paradox. The market's appetite for logic engines has grown far faster than the efficiency improvements. What next for Moore's Law? Engineers today are deploying a suite of techniques in the pursuit of more "logic" density, speed, and efficiency. The approaches include clever designs, embedding software within the logic engine itself, and using new materials to make transistors still smaller. There are also, as noted earlier, the entirely new classes of super-efficient silicon engines, the GPUs and Neural Processing Units (NPUs). The latter are analogous to how aerospace engineers invented jet engines to displace propellers in order to break the sound barrier – leading to more air travel and more fuel use.

Trends in the cost of logic, however, may be even more informative than the cost or efficiency of transistors *per se*. As we discussed briefly above, clever mathematics accelerate logic engine performance, and clever techniques, tools, and materials simultaneously reduce fabrication

Data is a resource that – unlike its natural analogues – humanity literally creates by inventing tools to sense and measure things.

costs. That combination is potent. In the 1960s mainframe era, $1,000 bought about one calculation per second. By 2000, $1 bought 10,000 calculations per second. Today $1 buys one billion calculations per second. (All in constant dollar terms.)

How much processing power might society ultimately consume? Data and information constitute a feature of our universe that is, like the universe itself, essentially infinite. Our appetite for data to gain greater knowledge and control of our world is limitless.

Last year saw the sixtieth anniversary of the logic engine. To gauge how early we are in this era, consider that 1936 was the sixtieth anniversary of the invention of the internal combustion engine. How much growth in demand for logic, for bytes, might the next few decades bring, never mind the next sixty years?

Metrics for measuring the future: from Medieval barrels to AI's bytes

Measuring and counting things may be humanity's oldest skill. Historians think numbering began with the Sumerians in 4,000 BC. But the ancient Egyptians were the first to create a word (in fact, a hieroglyph) for the then–unimaginably large number of one million.

Measuring the activity associated with infrastructures is the single best way to illuminate trends for planning and forecasting – and, of course, for governments to levy taxes or fees. After all, the overall traffic is where we see the effect of the "invisible hand of the market" revealed from myriad opaque decisions made by individual consumers and businesses.

While the Cloud, like all infrastructures, is realized in hardware, its traffic is quite different in two important ways. Until now, the others' metrics involved counting concrete things: gallons, miles, tons, bushels, barrels, etc. And, until now, counting activities hasn't come close to exhausting the numbering nomenclature itself.

The unit used to measure traffic, the "byte," is not a physical thing but an idea representing data, a term created by an IBM computer scientist in 1956, the same year the term "artificial intelligence" was coined.

Annual global Cloud traffic is today counted at some 40 zettabytes, an impossibly large number to imagine.

But one can imagine the weight of things. So, just how much do 40 zettabytes weigh? After all, the physical realities – i.e., the hardware and the energy needed to power the equipment – are where the rubber meets the road.

The answer? About ten million tons. Thank Amazon for helping to frame this feature of the physics of information. The web giant launched a service called the "Snowmobile," a 33-ton, 45-foot-long semi-trailer truck chock-a-block with digital memory that can hold 100 petabytes (PB) of data and transport it from a customer's premise to the Amazon Cloud. (100 PB is roughly the data in one million smartphones.)

The service was created to deal with the rapid growth

in petabyte-class data owned by increasing numbers of organizations. But in order for a business to take advantage of the cost and performance from storing and processing in the Cloud, that data has to be transported to those remote hyperscale datacenters. It's one of those ineluctable and annoying realities of physics that data transport speeds are roughly one thousand times slower over distances of miles compared to meters. Transferring 100 PB to a remote Cloud on the best high-speed fiber network would take over two decades.

The Snowmobile, however, parked at a customer site can upload 100 PB in about a week. Of note, during the week it uploads, the Snowmobile's digital hardware consumes electricity equivalent to about 40 barrels of oil, and then about another 10 barrels of actual oil driving the truck to a Cloud datacenter.

Now, to make useful forecasts about how much more data markets will yet generate and consume, we need a picture of the nature of data. The ancient Egyptians compiled data about grain storage and the like because it enabled planning. The Romans developed the census in order to lend precision to tax collection. Both forms of data collection have been central to civilization for eons.

Silicon technologies make it feasible to track materials from mine-mouth to factory to consumer – and not just in

Everything about the present and future digital infrastructure, especially its aggregate energy appetite, is captured at the intersection of extremes: the withering decline in the nanoscopic energy used per byte and the scale and blistering growth in bytes consumed.

terms of gross quantity, but also in real-time metrics such as location, temperature, velocity, wear rates, etc. Thus modern data collection not only includes, say, the number of people visiting a hospital or a number of cars transiting a city, but also real-time data such as each individual's specific location or activity (standing, sleeping, moving, heart rate), or the location, speed, and operational health of every car, and increasingly, any machine or device.

Then there is data about the data itself. Think of this as analogous to financial derivatives. Just as there is information to be gleaned from the velocity and volume of financial transactions without regard to the specifics of any transaction (e.g., the direction and speed of changes in the stock market), so too is there useful information in the "digital exhaust" from data collection and processing. This metadata is increasingly valuable as digital systems scale in both reach and granularity.

Data today is as different from that of the pre-digital

world as synthetic products like plastics, pharmaceuticals, and gasoline are different from natural products such as wood, paper, and grain.

Estimating the source and magnitude of prospective byte traffic reveals a lot about the shape of the future. But it may not tell us everything relevant about economic and social impacts. An air-mile has profoundly different utility than a car-mile or horse-mile. Similarly, a kilowatt-hour used to heat water is profoundly different from one used to spin a motor or light up a silicon engine. While such differences are particularly difficult to measure in digital domains, they are nonetheless anchored in counting bytes.

Data is the new oil

The popular turn of phrase "data is the new oil," credited to the U.K. mathematician and data scientist Clive Humby, of course leads to the observation that oil and data are different in an obvious way: one produces while the other uses energy. But that's not the point of the analogy. Twentieth century prosperity was fueled by petroleum and the myriad products and services that emerged from the automobile and the infrastructures of "personal mobility." Similarly, refining raw data leads to the even greater array of products and services that will spur growth in the twenty-first century.

Global Internet traffic is today about 10 *million* fold greater than when Amazon was founded in 1994. Could the next quarter century see a data explosion as great, or greater than, the last? And what would we call that era? We can frame an answer to the first question by considering macro trends.

Data is a resource that – unlike its natural analogues – humanity literally creates by inventing tools to sense and measure things. In a kind of virtuous circle, digital technologies themselves make possible better and even entirely new kinds of measuring tools.

Sensors range from the tiny GPS and accelerometer chips in every smartphone to monstrously sized scientific instruments like the Square Kilometer Array radio telescope. They all generate enormous scales of data about things that are both mundane, such as traffic patterns of cities and goods, and nearly theological, such as the shape of our universe. (The latter may lead to foundational knowledge that will, one day, change the world as much as the discovery of electromagnetism; but that's a subject for another time.) The Internet of Things entails much more than smart home thermostats, refrigerators, and roadways, but also innovations like sensor dust that can be sprayed onto agriculture fields for smart irrigation.

The physics of detection – acquiring and measuring data – is quite unlike the physics of information processing. Detectors and sensor tech have advanced even more rapidly than the technologies of logic. One can even "trick" nature to give up data by using the features of the phenomenon one is measuring. Engineers can literally chase measurements down to "the bottom" of nature with capabilities that seem genuinely magical. Scientists recently demonstrated a sensor capable of measuring motion at a thousandth the diameter of an atomic nucleus. Such a sensor can, in effect, "listen" to the motion of individual bacteria.

Or consider the implications of the cryo-EM, an astonishing new class of microscope whose inventors won a 2017 Nobel prize and allows, for the first time, direct imaging of biological structures at molecular scales. It's as big a leap as the invention of the optical microscope four hundred years earlier. The cyro-EM will similarly open new frontiers in biology – and a single cryo-EM generates petabyte levels of data.

It's in biological domains where we will find the single biggest vector for data generation. Few doubt that digitalization and software will yet unlock enormous medical cost efficiencies. But far more interesting are tomorrow's diagnostics and magical new cures that can only emerge from sensors, digital tools, and computing. The associated explosion in data collection will be epic. Genomic data alone is on track to generate as much as 40,000 PB a year. Then there's the concept of a virtual physiological human (VPH), the idea of "digital twin" for humans modeled on the same concept as for mechanical machines and industrial processes.

The pursuit of a VPH is currently focused on facilitating fundamental research and virtual clinical trials "*in silico*" for therapeutics within a supercomputer instead of within a human population. Once perfected, this will radically accelerate the time between discovery of a new therapeutic and its validation. Such VPHs will necessarily entail hundreds – and more likely thousands – of petabytes of data. In due course, the possibility that *everyone* will want their own personal digital twin in the Cloud is no more fantastical than thinking in 1980 that two billion people would one day carry more compute power in their pockets than a city's worth of IBM mainframes of that day.

The VPH also highlights the symbiosis with the proliferation of distributed sensors. A VPH will necessarily require collecting an individual's real-time body chemistry and biological data, ultimately down to individual organs and even, in theory, specific cells. Such sensors are now emerging from the field of biocompatible and "transient" electronics that enable not only wearable computing (e.g., smart Band-Aid–like sensors), but also consumable or even injectable smart therapeutics. A future where a billion people each own a petabyte-class VPH in the Cloud would generate thousands of zettabytes.

None of the above counts the flood of data from industrial sensors and industrial digital twins along with increasing automation in all the world's physical operating systems. Terabytes of data are already generated by the sensors on an aircraft's engine on each flight – with hundreds of thousands of flights a day – to improve maintenance and safety. And long before we see the autonomous car, the "connected" car with all its attendant safety and convenience features will generate terabytes per day per car. With two billion cars in the near future, that trend, arithmetically, eventually leads to zettabytes per *day*, not per year.

Of course all trends eventually face saturation. But there is no prospect for peak data in the foreseeable future. We are far further from saturation in data production than the world was in 1919 with oil production.

Traffic on the Internet already peaks at around one Snowmobile's worth of data every 30 seconds, and Cisco forecasts that total data traffic will rise more than fourfold in just a few years. That means we are quickly approaching 1,000 zettabytes – the yottabyte, which is the last official name for a really big number. To come up with names for yet bigger numbers, many computer scientists have unofficially endorsed the deliciously named brontobyte (1,000 yottas), and the geopbyte, (1,000 brontos). Sadly, the official international organization responsible for acceptable nomenclature is, with bureaucratic predictability, proposing pedantic alternative names.

Thus we come to the law of large numbers, and to the point of our excursion into the arcana of numerology. Everything about the present and future digital infrastructure, especially its aggregate energy appetite, is captured at the intersection of extremes: the withering decline in the nanoscopic energy used per byte and the scale and blistering growth in bytes consumed.

Processing a single byte entails an energy cost measured in nanojoules, itself an impossibly small number. A single flea hop entails 100 nanojoules. But process or move a byte a billion times per second – a gigahertz CPU – and transport those bytes a "bronto" times and you quickly aggregate to quantities of electricity greater than that consumed by any nation on earth.

It took sixty years to reach zettabytes of data generation, and now we'll add 1,000 times more than that before a decade passes. That flood of data, measured in yotta-bytes, will bring new services, products, and companies. This will be both surprising and truly exciting, and it will, overall, improve wellbeing. But all those benefits will derive from refining the raw data, all of which always consumes energy.

Perhaps credit for the aphorism that "data is the new oil" really belongs to Steve Jobs. His phrasing was a little less pithy, but the energy analogy finds its origins in a prescient lecture delivered by Jobs at Sweden's Lund University in 1985, when he said:

> [W]e're living in the wake of the last revolution, which was a new source of free energy. That was the free energy of petrochemicals. It completely transformed society, and we're products of this petrochemical revolution, which we're still living in the wake of today. We are now entering another revolution of free energy. A Macintosh uses less power than a few of those light-bulbs, yet can save us a few hours a day or give us a whole new experience. It's free "intellectual energy." [emphasis added]

In the context of infrastructures, Job's analogy could be reframed as a transition from the era of distributed connected computing, to one of ambient computing-centric services. It is a distinction with a difference.

And Jobs was right that the "intellectual energy" extracted by refining data and democratizing computing would be as revolutionary in economic and social terms as the advent of petrochemical engines. One suspects Jobs knew that his rhetorical flourish about "free energy" was hyperbole.

Everything, including the "intellectual energy" of AI and robots, has a physical energy cost. In the universe we live in, it always will.

First American edition published in 2019 by Encounter Books,
an activity of Encounter for Culture and Education, Inc.,
a nonprofit, tax exempt corporation.
Encounter Books website address: www.encounterbooks.com

Manufactured in the United States and printed on acid-free paper.
The paper used in this publication meets the minimum requirements of
ANSI/NISO Z39.48–1992 (R 1997) (*Permanence of Paper*).

FIRST AMERICAN EDITION

LIBRARY OF CONGRESS CATALOGING-IN-PUBLICATION DATA
IS AVAILABLE

10 9 8 7 6 5 4 3 2 1